MW01609945

LIFETRACERS
Conquer Your Past & Create Your Legacy

STEP 3: Processing Life Events

Authored By
Knox Gabriel

ISBN: 978-0-692-75357-6

Release Version:
Version 1.0

Published and Distributed By
TruthRocket Inc.
email: sales@TruthRocket.com

Designed by
TruthRocket Inc.

Graphics and Illustrations by
TruthRocket Inc.

Edited by
TruthRocket Inc.

STEP 3 - CONTENTS

HOW TO PROCESS LIFE EVENTS 5

    HOW YOUR MIND WORKS 5

    THE LOWER MIND 8

    OUR THOUGHTS CREATE OUR EMOTIONS 11

    THE EFFECT OF EMOTIONS ON OUR BODY 12

    THE ROLE OF FEAR IN OUR MIND 14

    INCREASING AWARENESS OF THOUGHTS AND EMOTIONS 20

COMING BACK TO CENTER 27

    PROCESSING YOUR THOUGHTS WISELY 42

    LEARNING FROM LIFE 45

    WHY IS LIFE SO HARD? 46

    THE DIFFERENCE BETWEEN PAIN AND SUFFERING 47

    USING DEATH AS A REFERENCE POINT 49

EMBRACING LIFE 52

    USING THE REWIND BUTTON IN YOUR LIFE 53

    FINALLY LETTING GO 55

    UNDERSTANDING OTHERS 57

NEXT STEPS 61

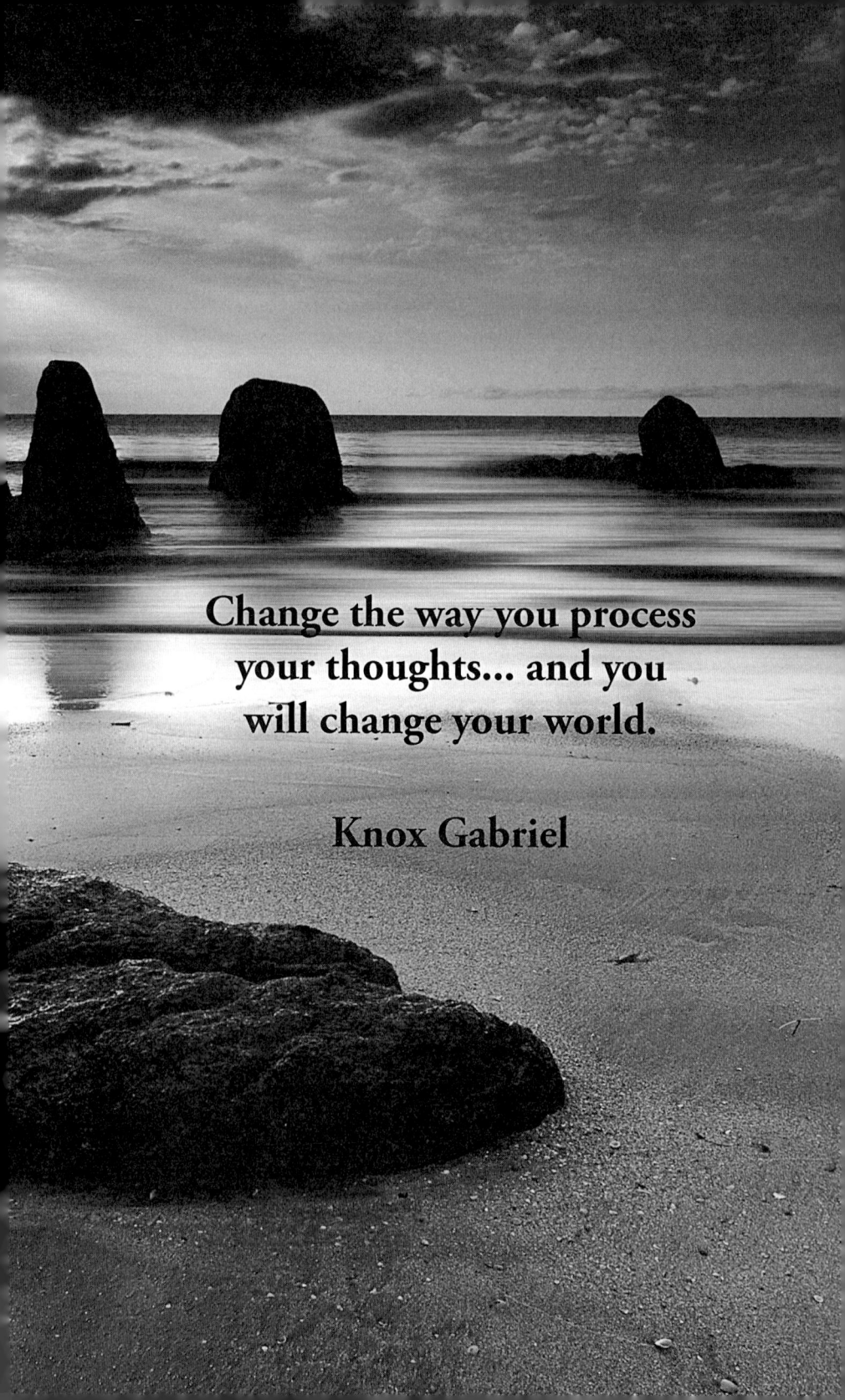

Change the way you process
your thoughts... and you
will change your world.

Knox Gabriel

How To Process Life Events

Up to this point in the course, we've been exploring how we use LifeTrace Charts and the LifeTracers' process to understand events that occur and what analysis of these events might tell us about you as a person.

From this point forward, we are going to be go internal (deep inside your mind) to help you gain a deeper understanding of how most people respond to life events within their mind and why this approach is not healthy. We are also going to be showing you some practical techniques you can use to respond to life events in different ways than you have in the past.

As we've already discussed, life events are part of the rhythm of life and there is nothing you can do to prevent them from happening. As a result, the best thing you can do is to embrace these events and to process them in a way that allows you to live a healthy, productive and purposeful life.

The methods and techniques included here are designed to be practical and common sense approaches to handling the emotional and mental aspects of processing life events. Once you read about these techniques and consider them in your mind, they will become so common sensical that you will ask yourself why you've lived your life in any other way. This should be a part of the journey of life for each of us...to find things that just make sense to us and that ring true inside our soul.

These methods and techniques should also be something you can implement in your life regardless of your religious or philosophical background and regardless of age or educational background. My goal was to make them as simple and straight-forward as possible so that anyone can put them into practical use.

How Your Mind Works

Your mind is a vast and wonderous thing. It sometimes seems impossible that all the wonderful things that can be accomplished with your mind are created by a small organ inside your skull (your brain). However, for all the wonderful things your mind can create and accomplish, there also millions of things that are not so wonderful that your mind does on a daily basis.

Most people don't realize that there are two distinct parts of the mind. Not only are they distinct and separate from one another but they also serve two entirely different purposes. This is not just some form of mythology or philosophy, it is a fact that has been known for thousands of years and has been put into practice by some of the most intelligent and highly evolved people that have ever walked the earth. The problem is that there are so few people who know about this and put it into practice that it is not something that is talked about or discussed by most people.

You may have heard some people say that we use less than 10% of our brain. So far, I haven't come across any scientific evidence to support this statement. However, it is clear that our brains have advanced capabilities that most of us never tap into. One of these advanced capabilities is something that I call our "Higher Mind". Most of us spend all day, every day, listening to and responding to our "Lower Mind". We'll talk in great detail about why this is not only a bad idea but it is very unhealthy and unproductive.

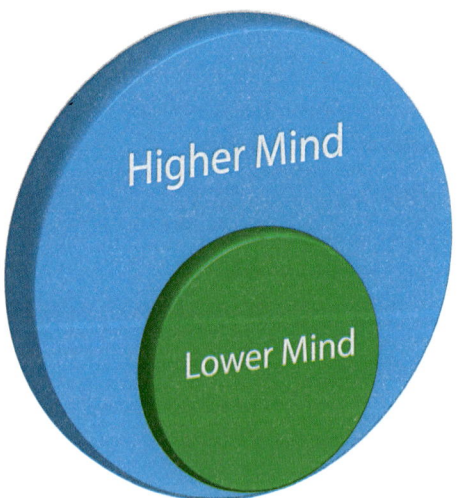

Figure 5.1

But before we get into that, let me just talk briefly about these names I've assigned to these two parts of our mind...."Higher Mind" and "Lower Mind". There is a specific reason I selected these names for each part of the mind. I have studied psychology, philosophy and religions from all around the world and I've heard these two things called many different names. I've also seen and heard people get into arguments about what these two parts should be called and what those names really mean. These arguments or disagreements are usually based on each person's philosophical or religious bias. People from one school of philosophy will call it one thing while people from a different religious background will call it something else.

Even the origins of this concept is something people will disagree and argue about. Some say it came from a famous philosopher, others credit it to one or more psychologists, while others claim is it part of an ancient or modern religion. To borrow a phrase from a famous movie "Frankly, my dear, I don't give a damn!". What I am most interested in is how do I effectively teach this concept to people from all walks of life so that they can put this powerful principal into practice in their own lives (particularly as it relates to life events). I have used this principal in my own life and have seen others use it very successfully as well. I know that it works and it is the only effective way I have found to truly deal with the deep emotional pain and trauma caused by major life events.

I have witnessed some of the most highly "religious" people in our society fail miserably at dealing with life events because they were attempting to use some of their own misplaced beliefs rather than using this process. Our history books are also filled with examples of highly intelligent psychologists, philosophers and authors who failed so miserably at dealing with life events that they chose to end their own life (a clear example of not following these principles).

So, if for any reason, you are hung up on the names I've assigned to these distinct parts of your mind…feel free to come up with your own names. At one point I was considering names such as "Laurel and Hardy", "Abbot and Costello", "Moe and Curly", "Jekyll and Hyde", "Andy (Griffith) and Don (Knotts)", "Ethel and Lucy", "Mary Ann and Ginger", "Spock and Kirk", "Beauty and the Beast" or "Sheldon (Cooper) and Amy (Farrah-Fowler)". I think you get the idea. So, seriously, you can call them whatever you want as long as you put these principals into practice in your own life.

What is most important to understand is that one of these parts of our mind (the "Higher Mind") represents the highest form of our self...the part that is evolved, aware, conscious, intelligent, observant and focused on our higher purpose in life. The other part of our mind (the "Lower Mind") represents the lowest part of our self...the part that is unevolved, unaware, unconscious and focused on constantly generating random thoughts that send us on endless goose chases, emotional roller coasters and foolish endeavors.

The Lower Mind is the part I am going to talk about first...because it is the part that most of us use all day every day... and the part that causes us the most trouble.

The Lower Mind

Have you ever wondered where all those voices in your head come from? All those voices that are constantly talking to you, moving swiftly from one topic to the next:

- The voice that talks to you about everything you see, hear, smell, touch and feel
- The voice that talks about all the people you come in contact with
- The voice that judges people within seconds of observing them
- The voice that is constantly wondering why bad things happen to you while good things are happening to other (less deserving) people
- The voice that tells you you're fat, ugly, stupid, unliked, unrespected or uncared for
- The voice that wants revenge when people do bad things to you.

All of these voices (and many more) are created by your Lower Mind. Your Lower Mind never stops. It uses up enormous amounts of energy creating an endless stream of thoughts about everything that is going on in our lives.

Have you ever wondered why there is always a voice that is narrating your entire life? Even if you are just walking through the park there is always that voice with something to say:

- "Look at that squirrel"
- "Wow…it looks like it might rain"
- "Look at that man asleep on the bench… I wonder if he's dead?"
- "Why is it that dogs always look like their masters?"
- "I could sure use a hamburger and fries right now".

Our brain contains the most powerful microprocessor that has ever been created. It can process something we see with our eyes into trillions of pixels in a matter of nanoseconds and immediately recognize the finest details within that image. It can process sounds perceived by our ears down to the smallest decibel levels and immediately recognize these sounds and interpret their meaning. It can also immediately recognize smells from our nose and sensory sensations from the nerve endings all over our body. It automatically knows when we're hungry, thirsty, tired or sleepy. Our brain doesn't need anyone to "tell it" what is going on. It already knows all these things.

So, why does our Lower Mind feel the need to "narrate" everything that is going on around us? Why does it feel the need to make arbitrary and sometimes false judgments about things... when our brain has already processed all these things a thousand times faster and more accurately than our Lower Mind can narrate them? If there is something going on around us that is actually a threat to us in any way, our brain will automatically trigger defense mechanisms within our body. We don't need some CNN or FOX announcer telling us what to think or what to do.

So why does our Lower Mind feel the need to do this? The reality is our Lower Mind is always looking for something to do… always looking for something to process… always looking for another way to consume energy.

Our Lower Mind is similar to the microprocessor inside your mobile phone. It is always running… always consuming energy (unless of course you turn it off). Even then it is sometimes still running in the background just in case it comes up with an excuse to turn on the phone and do something. Imagine if you gave your mobile phone to your child or teenager and gave them free reign over that phone. What would they do? They would most likely install about a thousand apps. Each of these apps would automatically turn on their respective GPS tracking feature so they can track you everywhere you go and send you endless notifications about why you should pay attention to whatever they are trying to sell you. Meanwhile, the microprocessor (your Lower Mind) is busy processing all the notifications from these apps and facilitating the process of sending you all these messages…which means it is also draining your battery of whatever energy remains since the last time you recharged the battery.

This is the primary reason that I try to install very few apps on my phone (and certainly don't give my children free reign over my phone). If you only have a few "useful" apps on your phone you will be amazed how long your battery will last…and how productive you will be because you are not always having to respond to endless notification messages from all those apps.

This is just one of many analogies I could use to describe how our Lower Mind works. We will talk about this more later in this chapter. But one thing you need to begin to understand…the more you step back and observe all the things your Lower Mind is doing and saying to you… the more you will realize just how useless (and sometimes down right ridiculous) your Lower Mind is. I won't go so far as to say that all thoughts produced by your Lower Mind are useless and ridiculous. But you will find that the greatest majority of them truly are.

Our Thoughts Create Our Emotions

We have already discussed how our Lower Mind creates many thoughts for us to process each day. But most people don't realize that each of these thoughts creates its own set of emotions. Your Lower Mind can create literally thousands of thoughts in a single day and each of these thoughts can generate its own set of emotions (sometimes more than one). This means that we may feel thousands of emotions in a single day. Is it any wonder that some of us just become emotional basket cases on certain days?

Figure 5.2

Positive thoughts are certainly capable of producing positive emotions (like happiness, surprise, joy and love). Yet, we spend most of our time and energy processing negative thoughts and the negative emotions (sadness, anger, disgust and fear) created by these thoughts.

Let's face it. When we are happy or feel loved, we enjoy that for a few moments and then we generally move on with our day. Seldom do we allow ourselves the time and freedom to truly dwell in these positive emotions throughout the entire day. But when we experience a negative emotion (such as sadness, anger or fear) it stays on our mind all day and sometimes for days and weeks at a time. Negative emotions consume so much of our personal energy and mind share that there is seldom time or space to focus on fleeting positive emotions.

The Effect Of Emotions On Our Body

We have discussed how the thoughts and emotions created by the Lower Mind can dominate our thought processes and feelings, but most people don't realize the damaging effect this can have on our body as well.

Each time our Lower Mind creates a thought and we choose to entertain or process that thought, our brain will send signals to our body to release certain chemicals or hormones within our body according to the type of thoughts and emotions being processed.

If we are processing positive thoughts, our brain sends signals to our body to release chemicals or hormones which give us that euphoric feeling of happiness, joy or excitement. Conversely, when we are processing negative thoughts, our brain sends signals to our body to release chemicals causing us to feel stress, fear, anxiety and depression.

There is a great deal of research being done in this area to better understand exactly what part of the brain triggers the release of the chemicals in the body. There are also differences of opinions as to when this occurs within the timeline of processing thoughts and emotions. However, one thing is clear…the more we continue to focus and dwell on particular thoughts and emotions the levels of hormones released into our body increases.

If we continually dwell on happy thoughts, our level of happy hormones increases. This actually improves our overall health, energy levels and slows down the aging process.

In contrast, if we continue to focus and dwell on negative thoughts, the increased levels of stress, fear and anxiety can do major damage to our health. Increased stress levels have been shown to increase inflammation throughout the body and accelerate the aging process.

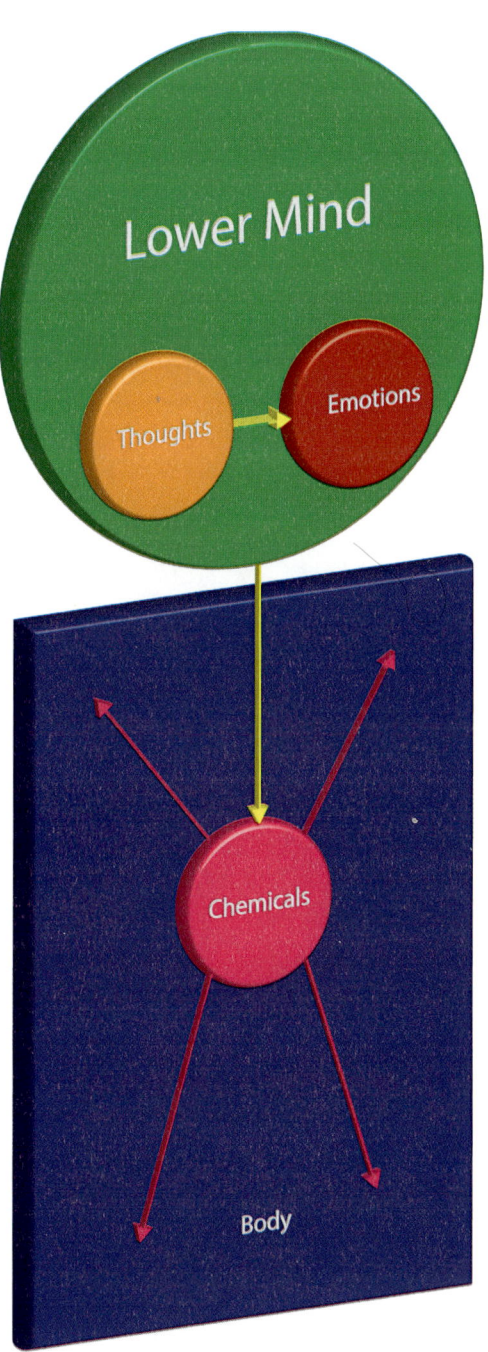

Figure 5.3

The Role Of Fear In Our Mind

Most of us don't realize the dominant role that fear plays in our mind. When we are experiencing negative emotions and someone asks us what is wrong… we will typically tell them we are sad, angry, disappointed or disgusted. But if that person were to dive a little deeper and ask us "why" we are feeling these negative emotions, more often than not the true answer is because we are afraid or fearful of something.

For instance, when in a relationship we will sometimes find ourselves feeling sad. But the real reason we are feeling sad is because we are fearful that:

- This person doesn't really love us
- They might leave us
- We might not be able to continue loving them.

At other times, we find ourselves feeling angry. But the real reason we are angry is because someone did something that made us feel rejected, not respected, jealous or perhaps threatened. All these feelings derive from different fears:

- Fear of being rejected
- Fear of not being respected
- Fear of loss or
- Fear that something hurtful which happened in our past might happen again.

The more aware I become of the role that fear plays in our lives, the more I see it in people everywhere I go:

- The man or woman who gets jealous when they think their significant other is flirting with someone (fear of loss)
- The way we make decisions based on what our family, friends and society might think about us (fear of rejection or fear of not being respected)
- Someone who resists or avoids entering into intimate relationships (fear of being hurt or abused)

- Someone who reacts out of pride related to money or possessions (fear of loss and fear of not being respected).

Because all these emotions are based on different deep seated fears, most people think these emotions are automatic, uncontrollable and undeniable. They seem to just automatically fire off in certain situations. These situations act as trigger points (just like the trigger on a gun).

Wouldn't we live in a crazy and scary world if every one of us walked around with a gun... with our finger constantly on the trigger (just waiting to fire away). While this sounds like a scary world, it would actually be safer than the world we live in now. When someone carries a gun, there are several decisions that have to be made before someone actually pulls the trigger:

1. Am I in a situation where I might need to use my gun to protect myself?
2. What are the potential consequences of pulling the trigger (to myself and others)?
3. Is it really worth it to me to pull the trigger?
4. Am I going to pull the trigger?

This series of decisions makes us stop, evaluate and think before we pull the trigger. However, when dealing with emotions (especially fear-based emotions) most of us don't consciously do any of these steps. Perhaps a few of us might take the time to do #1 and #4. But for most of us, these reactions are just "automatic". It's as if we are walking around with an automatic weapon just waiting for an opportunity to let it blast away.

Unfortunately, it is only after we blast away at people (metaphorically) that we then take time to reflect and ask the questions:

1. Was I really in a situation where I needed to react out of fear to protect myself?
2. What are the consequences (to myself and others) now that I've reacted fearfully?
3. Was it really worth it to express all that fear and anger?

4. Why do I always react that way?

At each point along the way, there are decisions that are being made. However, we have been reacting this way ever since we were a child and these decisions have become (seemingly) automatic. Let's break this down step by step:

1. Was I really in a situation where I needed to react out of fear to protect myself?

    The first step here is to STOP long enough to RECOGNIZE the situation. Most of us never stop to recognize or evaluate the situation, we just react. This is the most important step in the entire process. This will take time and practice to retrain your mind (and we will discuss specific techniques for this a little later) but each time a situation (trigger point) happens we have to train ourselves to STOP (mentally) and recognize that there is a trigger point here and we will need to make some decisions rather than just firing away automatically.

    The second step is to RECOGNIZE which fear inside of us is being triggered. Why am I angry, sad, disappointed or afraid? As you practice this, you will begin to quickly recognize the fear that is driving your reaction:

    • I'm fearful of losing this person

    • I'm fearful of being alone

    • I'm fearful of not being respected

    • I'm fearful of losing my status (financially or otherwise).

    The third step is to RECOGNIZE whether this fear is valid and necessary. In the majority of the cases the answer will be "No". Once you truly understand these fears in relation to who you are as a person (a complete and perfect person), you will see clearly that most fears in your life are totally unnecessary. In fact, you will begin to see just how ridiculous these fears are.

2. What are the consequences (to myself and others) if I react fearfully?

Most of us don't fully appreciate and respect the power that is contained within the words we speak to others. Our tongues are the most powerful weapon we have on our bodies.

> *"Death and life are in the power of the tongue: and they that love it shall eat the fruit thereof."*   King James Bible (Proverbs 18:21)

There is nothing more powerful than speaking a positive word to someone. Your words may serve as motivation for that person for a lifetime. However, nothing is more devastating than a negative word spoken out of anger. The devasting effect of your words on another person's life will linger indefinitely in their mind.

Once you have pulled the trigger (and released these words) the damage you created cannot be undone. It may be forgiven by that person…but it will never be forgotten.

In most parts of the world, people have the right to own a gun and to shoot that gun whenever they want (as long as they are not posing a threat to other people). However, they don't have the right to destroy the lives of other people with this weapon.

Our world is filled with people who speak first and then think. They feel they have the right to speak whatever is on their mind (and they do have this right in the right environment and in a constructive way). However, they don't have the right to go around destroying the lives of others with their tongue anymore than they have the right to go around shooting others with their bullets.

Living in a life of fear and reacting based on those fears will destroy all the relationships that you hold so dear. We've already talked about the impact we can have on other people when we react out of fear. Yet one of the greatest fears for most people is the fear of being alone in this world. When you live out of fear and react out of fear you are creating a self-fulfilling prophecy. It is only a matter of time before no one will want to be around you…because they will grow tired of being a potential target for your angry outbursts.

3.   Was it really worth it to express all of that fear and anger?

Once you begin to understand how ridiculous most of your fears are…you will quickly realize this is no way to live your life. The damage that you do to yourself and to the lives of people all around you is simply too great of a cost to live your life this way.

4.   Why do I always react that way?

The problem is not that we react to our fears. Reacting to a fear is a process that occurs naturally within our bodies.

The problem is that we are allowing our mind to dwell and focus on the thoughts that create these fears. When we dwell and focus on these negative thoughts we provide energy to them.

A stick of dynamite is not dangerous. Lighting it is dangerous.
Knox Gabriel

Once you light a stick of dynamite you have provided it with energy. It is only a matter of time until it explodes. When it explodes it destroys itself and potentially many other things around it.

Negative thoughts are just like sticks of dynamite. They are not dangerous until you apply energy to them. Your Lower Mind continuously produces thoughts of all kinds. But that doesn't mean you have to dwell and focus on these thoughts (thus providing them with the energy to explode). The goal is to (1) recognize the type of thought it is, (2) process the thought as quickly as possible, and (3) let go of it as quickly as possible.

We'll discuss this approach more in the next section.

Increasing Awareness Of Thoughts and Emotions

We've discussed at some length now how your Lower Mind is continuously producing thoughts which in turn create associated emotions. This process of producing thoughts and emotions is an endless cycle that is seemingly unstoppable. So, now that we know this, what can you do to more effectively manage this within your mind?

The good news is that you've already accomplished the first step in managing this process more effectively.

Step 1. Be Aware (Of Your Lower Mind)

Now that you know what your Lower Mind is doing, this step should be easy. Right? While this step is simple and easy, it is something that will require practice. You have 20, 30 or 40+ years of bad habits that need to be broken and retrained. This won't happen overnight and you will find yourself slipping back into your old ways of thinking from time to time.

But the important thing is to stay diligent. Come back and reread these steps frequently. Better yet…go to our website and print out the "4 Steps To Awareness" infographic and put it up on your wall as a reminder:

http://KnoxGabriel.com/4StepsToAwareness

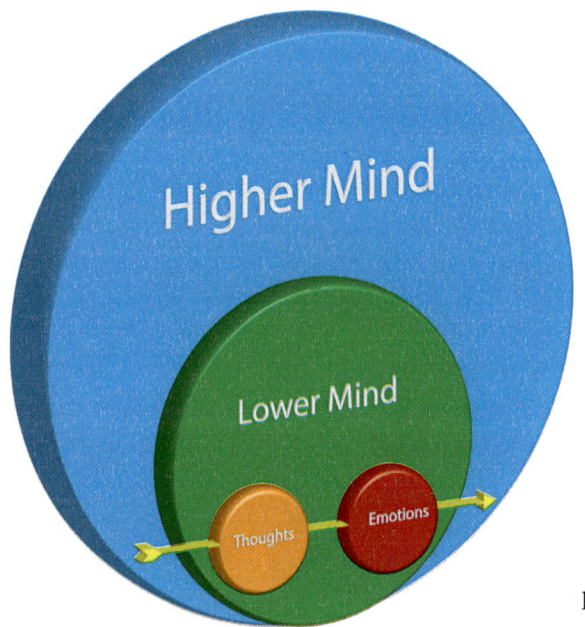

Figure 5.4

Right now, I want you to do some practicing with me. Do the following:

- Turn off your TV, radio, cell phone or anything else that might interrupt you.

- Sit down in a quiet, still place.

- Look at the image in Figure 5.4 above and imagine yourself taking one step backward from your Lower Mind. You are now residing in your Higher Mind. Now take one step up in your mind (kind of like going up one step on the bleachers at a game to give you a better view).

- Begin to quietly listen and observe all the thoughts being created by your mind. Take 3 - 5 minutes to just listen to and observe these thoughts. Don't act on them… just listen.

- No really! Do it now!

- [3 - 5 minute pause]

Isn't it amazing the endless stream of thoughts that occur? You probably heard thoughts that went something like this:

1. "OK. This process seems silly…but I'll try it anyway."

2. "How long is 3 - 5 minutes?" "How will I know when to stop?" "Maybe I should set a timer on my phone?"

3. "OK…I'm waiting…where's my first thought?"

4. "Oh man…I just remembered…I need to go to the store. I'll do that later."

5. "What am I going to do this weekend?"

6. "That reminds me I need to return that phone call."

7. "Oh look…something shiny!"

8. "I wonder if this process really works."

9. "Am I really controlled by my thoughts?"

10. "Can I actually observe my thoughts from a distance?"

11. "Wouldn't that be cool if I could just watch my life from a different perspective?"

12. "Squirrel? Was that a squirrel I just saw outside the window?"

13. "Oh yeah…I'm supposed to be observing my thoughts?"

14. "Man…I'm getting hungry."

15. "I sure could use a glass of wine right now."

16. "Is it time to stop observing my thoughts? No… still have more time."

17. "Wow…I really do produce a lot of thoughts!"

18. "You know…that still bugs me what Kelly said to me."

19. "I really didn't deserve that."

20. "I need to tell her how she made me feel."

21. "Oh…that makes me so angry!"

22. "What can I do to get back at her?"

23. "Maybe I should post something bad about her on social media."

24. "What about that secret that she told me? She would just die if I told people about that?"

25. "But that would definitely end our friendship. Maybe that's not such a good idea."

26. "I've spent years developing that friendship. I don't know what I'd do without her."

27. "But I am just so angry. I can't get my mind off of this."

28. "This whole thing just makes my stomach hurt. I really do feel sick."

29. "Squirrel! That really was a squirrel that time!"

30. "Wow…I really do produce a lot of thoughts!"

That's 30 thoughts in less than 3 minutes. As you can see, we produce a lot of thoughts. Since there are 960 "awake" minutes in the day (assuming you sleep 8 hours), that equates to 9,600 thoughts each day (using this primitive example). If you do some research, you will see estimates even higher than this (from 20,000 to as high as 80,000 thoughts per day). Now you can see why it is so important that we pay attention to how we process our thoughts.

But the most important thing is to learn and practice the process I've previously outlined. In fact, as you did this exercise, you completed Steps 2, 3 and part of Step 4. Let's look at what you just accomplished.

Step 2. Decide

In order to complete the exercise you just did, the first step you had to complete was to DECIDE that you weren't going to think the way you normally do. You had to DECIDE to take a different approach. This is a conscious decision you will need to practice making many times throughout your day. Eventually, this will become your new default way of thinking. But for now, you will need to constantly remind yourself to make this decision.

Step 3: Step Back, Step Up and Observe

Once you made the decision to process your thoughts differently, you took action to STEP BACK away from your Lower Mind and to STEP UP to give you a better perspective on your thoughts. You positioned yourself in your Higher Mind so that you could objectively observe all the thoughts being created by your Lower Mind. In effect, you just removed yourself from the rat race of your own thoughts. The more you practice this and the more you learn to reside in this space of the Higher Mind…the more you will come to cherish this place in your mind.

Step 4: Recognize, Process and Let Go

If you had actually recorded (or written down) all of your thoughts during this time, you would have a list similar to the one I just used as an example. You would be able to go back through this list one by one and RECOGNIZE what type of thought each one is.

Most of the thoughts listed here are just trivial or silly thoughts. When we have these types of thoughts, we just naturally have them and then we LET GO of them. This seems like a normal thing for us to do. There is no value in holding onto these thoughts and it would just be a waste of energy to do so. There are also some "To Do" items on this list (things our mind remembers and reminds us of from time to time). This is why it's important to keep "To Do" lists. Once you write these things down in an actual "To Do List" your mind is less likely to waste energy recalling them for you.

Now go back and look at items #18 - #28 on this list (the thoughts about a friend named Kelly). These are thoughts based on an actual event. In this example, this event was a relatively minor event in comparison to other major life events we experience. But look at how much energy is being spent thinking about this one event. It is also clear from this example that this is something that has been thought about many times already and will continue to be thought about for some time to come. This person was obviously hurt by something that Kelly said. This has caused them to feel sad, angry and betrayed. But underlying these emotions is the core fear of losing this friendship (and perhaps being left alone).

These are the types of thoughts that we need to quickly RECOGNIZE, PROCESS and LET GO of.

In this example, you need to quickly RECOGNIZE that this is the type of negative event (and associated negative thoughts) that can literally eat you alive if you allow it to. Red flags should be going off in your head. Once you RECOGNIZE that these are negative thoughts, you will need to quickly PROCESS this thought. "Processing" this thought means reminding yourself that these thoughts are just perceptions based upon your past experiences and your core fears. In this example, it is the core fear of losing a friendship or possibly being alone that drives this thought process. However, to deal with this fear you will need to remind yourself of your true identity (which we covered in the previous section). You are a complete and perfect being and you don't need anything or anyone else to complete you. Once you reflect on your true identity you will be able to LET GO of this fear and LET GO of these negative thoughts.

Your power comes from your ability
to stay calm in the midst
of the storm.

Knox Gabriel

Coming Back To Center

Have you ever heard the term "coming back to center" or to "center yourself"? Have you ever wondered what that really means? Depending on the philosophies or religions you have studied in your life you may or may not have heard this term. But there are specific applications of this concept when it comes to dealing with life events.

Responding to the thoughts and emotions associated with life events is like living your life on a pendulum. You are constantly swinging from one extreme to the other. A pendulum follows one of the great laws of nature. Whatever distance a pendulum swings in one direction…it must also swing the same distance in the opposite direction. Another way of saying this is whatever energy is applied to the pendulum in one direction is the same amount of energy that will be applied to it in the other direction.

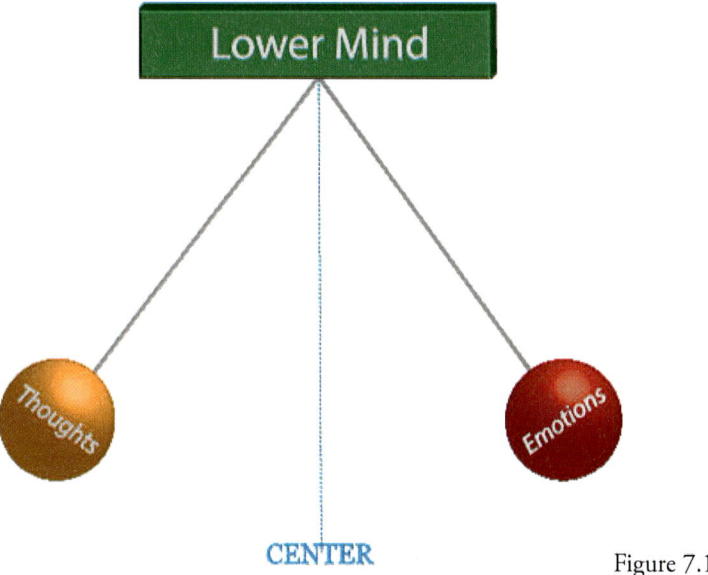

Figure 7.1

As we apply this principle to our life events, this means that whatever amount of energy you put into holding onto a thought associated with a life event… that is how much energy you will also have to put into dealing with the emotions on the other side of the pendulum from that thought. You are constantly expending countless amounts of energy dealing with one thought and then the associated emotions generated from that thought. Then you deal with another thought and the associated emotions generated from that thought.

In this pattern, you are simply wearing yourself out and it is impossible to accomplish anything real and meaningful in your life. It's like being on one of those swinging pirate boat rides at the state fair… but you can never get off the ride. The only way you can get off the ride is if you can convince the captain (the ride operator) to stop applying energy (electricity in this case) to the ride. But here is the good news…guess who the captain of this ship is? You are!

All you have to do is to make a decision that you are more interested in getting off the ride than you are continuing to apply energy to your thoughts and emotions. Guess what happens when you finally get off the ride? You are finally at rest…at peace. You have allowed yourself to come back to the center of the pendulum…the center of your life.

When you stop responding to the thoughts being created by your lower mind… you also stop having to deal with the emotions being created by those thoughts. If you don't entertain the thoughts… you don't have to entertain the emotions either. You have stopped adding energy to these thoughts and emotions.

Once you're off the ride…you can just sit there at peace. This doesn't mean the ride stops just because you are no longer on it. Your lower mind never stops creating thoughts and emotions. But since you are no longer on the ride… you can just sit there from a distance and observe the useless and wasteful thoughts and emotions being created by your lower mind. You are now observing them from a distance and not supplying them with any energy. You recognize that your lower mind is creating these thoughts and emotions… but you simply let them pass on by. Let's look at how this applies to some specific life events.

Life Event 1: Loss of Employment

What happens if you are suddenly laid off or terminated from your job? What is the first thing that happens? Your lower mind immediately goes into hyperdrive mode…creating negative thoughts and possibilities just as fast as it can process them:

- What am I going to do to make money?
- Where will I find another job?
- What if it takes six months or a year to find another job?
- What if I can't find another job at all?
- How will I pay the bills?
- How am I going to take care of my family?
- What if I'm evicted or don't have a place to live?
- What will people think about me?
- Will they judge me or think less of me because I don't have a job?

Each of these negative thoughts carries with it one or more associated negative emotions or states of mind (fear, anger, sadness, depression, anxiety). Your mind will be in constant motion (from one side of the pendulum to the other) processing each of these thoughts and emotions. When it gets to the end of the list it will start all over at the beginning of the list again…an endless cycle of wasted energy.

Life Event 2: Unfaithful Spouse / Significant Other

What if you just discovered that your spouse or significant other is having an affair? Your lower mind immediately goes back into hyperdrive mode… creating negative thoughts and possibilities about as fast as it can process them:

- How could they have done this to me?
- What did I do wrong to deserve this?
- Is there any way we can make it through this as a couple?
- What can I do to get back at them?

- Does this mean we should breakup or get a divorce?
- What will a divorce do to our finances?
- What will people think about me?
- Does this mean there is something wrong with me?
- Will anyone ever be faithful to me?
- Will anyone ever love me?

Once again, there are negative emotions created for each of these thoughts. Your lower mind will go over and over this list and constantly remind you of all the emotions you "should" be feeling. But remember, just because your lower mind generates these thoughts and emotions doesn't mean you have to go along for the ride. You can make a decision at any time to get off the ride and process these thoughts and emotions differently.

You may be asking yourself right now…how do I actually do that? This all sounds great but can I really stop listening to all these thoughts? Can I really stop feeling all these emotions?

Think about a professional actor. How can an actor play a tragic role within a play or film (perhaps even emoting negative thoughts and emotions to the camera or audience) without losing their true personal identity (off the set)? How can they remain a positive and conscious human being while playing these dramatic roles? It is because they know that each role is temporary… and they will soon release themselves from this role and continue on in their life with their true identity intact.

Just because you may temporarily play a role (in real life) as someone who is unemployed, divorced, abused, addicted or even someone who has lost a loved one… these roles are all temporary and they do not change who you truly are. They do not change your true identity as a complete and perfect creation.

Remember the 4 steps we outlined in the previous section for processing our thoughts and emotions:

Step 1. Be Aware (Of Your Lower Mind)

Step 2. Decide (To Use A Different Approach)

Step 3: Step Back, Step Up & Observe (Your Thoughts)

Step 4: Recognize, Process and Let Go (Of Your Thoughts & Emotions).

Assuming we've already stopped ourselves and implemented Steps 1 - 3 to begin observing our thoughts, let's take a closer look at how we would actually implement Step 4 to Recognize, Process and Let Go of some specific thoughts and emotions.

Let's go back to the Life Event #2 we listed above and go through how we can process these thoughts in a more efficient way. On the following pages we'll list each thought and talk through the specific steps to Process and Let Go of each thought.

[Note: you will see many steps repeated across these different thoughts. That is because there is a specific process you should go through on each of your thoughts. But there may be subtle differences on how to handle particular types of thoughts. Don't let the repetitiveness of this exercise turn you off. The repetitiveness is what you need to learn. You should be repeating this process in your head thousands of times a day.]

Life Event #2: Unfaithful Spouse/Significant Other

- **Thought: How could they have done this to me?**
  1. <u>Recognize</u> this is a "red flag" thought that may consume you if you provide energy to it.
  2. <u>Process</u> the thought quickly:
     a. Realize that this thought could easily make you feel negative emotions (anger, disappointment, fear, shame). It is even OK to feel these emotions briefly (just long enough to process them)
     b. Remind yourself that there is nothing about this thought (or its associated emotions) that changes your true identity
     c. Make a mental note to remind yourself that you won't ever be able to control the decisions or actions of others (you can only control your own decisions and actions).
  3. <u>Let Go</u> of the thought and emotions:
     a. Move back to center
     b. Focus on your true identity as a complete and perfect creation
     c. Create something positive. You are a creator by nature so use this experience to create something (a journal entry, a picture, a book, a song, a mental image of you in a better place, a plan for handling similar situations in the future).

- **Thought: What did I do wrong to deserve this?**
    1. <u>Recognize</u> this is a "red flag" thought that may consume you if you provide energy to it
    2. <u>Process</u> the thought quickly:
        a. Realize that this thought could easily make you feel negative emotions (anger, disappointment, fear, shame). It is even OK to feel these emotions briefly (just long enough to process them)
        b. Remind yourself that there is nothing about this thought (or its associated emotions) that changes your true identity
        c. Make a mental note to remind yourself that you won't ever be able to control the decisions or actions of others (you can only control your own decisions and actions). It is possible you did nothing wrong. Don't take ownership of someone else's decisions or actions. If you objectively feel you made a bad decision…then take ownership of your own decisions and actions. We all make poor decisions (from time to time) but this doesn't change our true identity. Make note of what you need to do differently in the future to make better decisions.
    3. <u>Let Go</u> of the thought and emotions:
        a. Move back to center
        b. Focus on your true identity as a complete and perfect creation
        c. Create something positive. You are a creator by nature so use this experience to create something (a journal entry, a picture, a book, a song, a mental image of you in a better place, a plan for handling similar situations in the future).

- **Thought: Is there any way we can make it through this as a couple?**

    1. <u>Recognize</u> this is a "red flag" thought that may consume you if you provide energy to it. While there is nothing inherently negative about this particular thought you do need to realize it is the type of thought that can consume you.

    2. <u>Process</u> the thought quickly:

        a. Realize that this thought could easily make you feel negative emotions (anger, disappointment, fear, shame). It is even OK to feel these emotions briefly (just long enough to process them)

        b. Remind yourself that there is nothing about this thought (or its associated emotions) that changes your true identity

        c. This particular thought can be used in a constructive way (perhaps along with counseling) to work towards a positive solution. Make a mental note to remind yourself that you won't ever be able to control the decisions or actions of others (you can only control your own decisions and actions). If the other party is expressing genuine interest in trying to work it out as a couple, then it is reasonable to formulate a plan to explore this option. You can only control your own decisions and actions. You will be OK no matter what happens because you are a complete and perfect person and you don't need someone else to complete you or fulfill you. Remember, don't let this thought process consume your thoughts or emotions.

    3. <u>Let Go</u> of the thought and emotions:

        a. Move back to center

        b. Focus on your true identity as a complete and perfect creation

        c. Create something positive. You are a creator by nature so use this experience to create something (a journal entry, a picture, a book, a song, a mental image of you in a better place, a plan for handling similar situations in the future).

- **Thought: What can I do to get back at them?**
  1. <u>Recognize</u> this is a major "red flag" thought that will consume you if you provide energy to it.
  2. <u>Process</u> the thought quickly:
     a. Realize that this thought is a time bomb of negative emotions (anger, disappointment, fear). You could easily waste enormous amounts of energy on this one thought. While it is OK to feel these emotions briefly (just long enough to process them), you need to be really careful with these particular emotions
     b. Remind yourself that there is nothing about this thought (or its associated emotions) that changes your true identity
     c. This is a very dangerous thought process which can be very destructive both to yourself and to others. Make a mental note to remind yourself that you won't ever be able to control the decisions or actions of others (you can only control your own decisions and actions). Then move on quickly.
  3. <u>Let Go</u> of the thought and emotions:
     a. Move back to center
     b. Focus on your true identity as a complete and perfect creation
     c. Create something positive. You are a creator by nature so use this experience to create something (a journal entry, a picture, a book, a song, a mental image of you in a better place, a plan for handling similar situations in the future).

- **Thought: Does this mean we should breakup or get a divorce?**

    1. <u>Recognize</u> this is a "red flag" thought that may consume you if you provide energy to it. Although this is a valid thought and there is nothing inherently negative about this particular thought, you do need to realize this is the type of thought that can consume you.

    2. <u>Process</u> the thought quickly:

        a. Realize that this thought could easily make you feel negative emotions (anger, disappointment, fear, shame). It is even OK to feel these emotions briefly (just long enough to process them)

        b. Remind yourself that there is nothing about this thought (or its associated emotions) that changes your true identity

        c. This particular thought can be used in a constructive way (perhaps to work toward reconciliation or to work toward an amicable dissolution of the relationship). Make a mental note to remind yourself that you won't ever be able to control the decisions or actions of others (you can only control your own decisions and actions). If the other party is expressing genuine interest in trying to work it out as a couple, then it is reasonable to formulate a plan to explore this option. You can only control your own decisions and actions. You will be OK no matter what happens because you are a complete and perfect person and you don't need someone else to complete you or fulfill you. Remember, don't let this thought process consume your thoughts or emotions.

    3. <u>Let Go</u> of the thought and emotions:

        a. Move back to center

        b. Focus on your true identity as a complete and perfect creation

        c. Create something positive. You are a creator by nature so use this experience to create something (a journal entry, a picture, a book, a song, a mental image of you in a better place, a plan for handling similar situations in the future).

- **Thought: What will people think about me?**
    1. <u>Recognize</u> this is a major "red flag" thought that will consume you if you provide energy to it. This thought is entirely based on your own pride (which is another way of saying your own fears).

    2. <u>Process</u> the thought quickly:
        a. Realize that this thought could easily make you feel negative emotions (anger, disappointment, fear, shame). It is even OK to feel these emotions briefly (just long enough to process them)

        b. Remind yourself that there is nothing about this thought (or its associated emotions) that changes your true identity. You are a complete and perfect person (regardless of the situation) and what other people may think of you will never change that

        c. There is nothing constructive about this thought (other than to remind you that you should never live your life based on what other people think). Make a mental note to remind yourself that you won't ever be able to control the thoughts or actions of others. You can only control your own thoughts and actions. You will be OK no matter what happens because you are a complete and perfect person and you don't need someone else's approval or opinion to complete you or fulfill you. Get rid of this thought as quickly as possible.

    3. <u>Let Go</u> of the thought and emotions:
        a. Move back to center

        b. Focus on your true identity as a complete and perfect creation

        c. Create something positive. You are a creator by nature so use this experience to create something (a journal entry, a picture, a book, a song, a mental image of you in a better place, a plan for handling similar situations in the future).

- **Thought: Does this mean there is something wrong with me?**

  1. <u>Recognize</u> this is a major "red flag" thought that will consume you if you provide energy to it. This thought is entirely based on your own fears.

  2. <u>Process</u> the thought quickly:

     a. Realize that this thought could easily make you feel negative emotions (anger, disappointment, fear, shame). It is even OK to feel these emotions briefly (just long enough to process them)

     b. Remind yourself that there is nothing about this thought (or its associated emotions) that changes your true identity. You are a complete and perfect person (regardless of the situation) and there is nothing wrong with you

     c. It is fairly normal to go through a period of self-evaluation in situations like this. But if you are going to conduct this self-evaluation…you need to do it from an objective viewpoint not based on your fears. You can honestly assess your strengths and weakness at any point in your life (this is a healthy process). But you should never conduct this process because you feel that you are somehow flawed or incomplete. You are who you are (strengths and weaknesses included). You will be OK no matter what happens because you are a complete and perfect person. But we should always be exploring ways to improve ourselves.

  3. <u>Let Go</u> of the thought and emotions:

     a. Move back to center

     b. Focus on your true identity as a complete and perfect creation

     c. Create something positive. You are a creator by nature so use this experience to create something (a journal entry, a picture, a book, a song, a mental image of you in a better place, a plan for improving yourself from a positive viewpoint).

- **Thought: Will anyone ever be faithful to me?**
  1. <u>Recognize</u> this is a major "red flag" thought that will consume you if you provide energy to it. This thought is entirely based on your own fears of being hurt again.
  2. <u>Process</u> the thought quickly:
     a. Realize that this thought could easily make you feel negative emotions (anger, disappointment, fear, shame). It is even OK to feel these emotions briefly (just long enough to process them)
     b. Remind yourself that there is nothing about this thought (or its associated emotions) that changes your true identity. You are a complete and perfect person (regardless of the situation) and there is nothing wrong with you
     c. This is a common reaction when someone is unfaithful. But you need to understand this reaction is based on your fears of being hurt again or fears of not being loved. But you will never be able to control the decisions and actions of others. You know this is an inherent risk of being in a relationship and you accept that risk because of the benefits that normally come with a relationship. People are often brought into our lives for a season and we never know how long that season will last. We should just be thankful and feel blessed for the time that we shared with them. We are each complete and perfect beings and don't need anyone else in our lives. Until you come to this realization, you will never be able to have a truly healthy relationship with someone else. Focus on being the best version of you. Focus on being the type of person that people naturally want to be around… and then watch as people are magnetically drawn to you because of your positive energy. But when they are drawn to you, don't make the mistake of falling back into the mindset that you "need" them… because you don't.
  3. <u>Let Go</u> of the thought and emotions:
     a. Move back to center

      b. Focus on your true identity as a complete and perfect creation

      c. Create something positive. You are a creator by nature so use this experience to create something (a journal entry, a picture, a book, a song, a mental image of you in a better place, a plan for improving yourself from a positive viewpoint).

- **Thought: Will anyone ever love me?**

  1. <u>Recognize</u> this is a major "red flag" thought that will consume you if you provide energy to it. This thought is entirely based on your own fears of being alone or fears of not being loved.

  2. <u>Process</u> the thought quickly:

      a. Realize that this thought could easily make you feel negative emotions (anger, disappointment, fear, shame). It is even OK to feel these emotions briefly (just long enough to process them)

      b. Remind yourself that there is nothing about this thought (or its associated emotions) that changes your true identity. You are a complete and perfect person (regardless of the situation) and there is nothing wrong with you

      c. This is a common reaction when someone is unfaithful. But you need to understand this reaction is based on fears of being alone or fears of not being loved. But the reality is…we all need to be perfectly OK with being alone. We are each complete and perfect without anyone else in our lives. If we live the rest of our lives without someone in our life…we should all be comfortable with that concept

      d. Until you come to this realization, you will never be able to have a truly healthy relationship with someone else. Focus on being the best version of you. Focus on being the type of person that people naturally want to be around…and then watch as people are magnetically drawn to you because of your positive energy. But when they are drawn to you…don't make the mistake of falling back into the mindset that you "need" them…because you don't.

3. <u>Let Go</u> of the thought and emotions:

    a. Move back to center

    b. Focus on your true identity as a complete and perfect creation

    c. Create something positive. You are a creator by nature so use this experience to create something (a journal entry, a picture, a book, a song, a mental image of you in a better place, a plan for improving yourself from a positive viewpoint).

Hopefully this process of going through these common questions and observing how we should be processing these thoughts and emotions is helpful. I realize that there is a lot of repetition in these answers. That is by design… because you need to develop a repetitive process (a way of observing and processing your thoughts) that you can easily remember and repeat. You will end up using this process hundreds or thousands of times in a day.

Once you become accustomed to using this process, you will see how your Lower Mind adapts and how you find yourself with additional time and energy to apply to more productive thought processes (as we discuss in the next section).

Processing Your Thoughts Wisely

In the previous section, we've been discussing how to process your thoughts quickly and more efficiently. One of the reasons we do this is to to avoid wasting so much time and energy on useless and wasteful thought processes. However, the more important reason we do this is to expand and maximize the amount of time and energy we have for pursuing more positive, creative and fulfilling thought processes.

As you begin to process the thoughts created by your Lower Mind more efficiently, you will begin to notice some extra space being created between your thoughts. You will literally say to yourself "Wow...I'm not having any thoughts right now"! As you begin to put this space to use wisely, the space between your lower thoughts will increase.

Your Lower Mind is just like a bully who wants attention. Once you start ignoring all its antics...it will become bored and produce these useless thoughts less frequently. Over time, you can train the Lower Mind to only produce thoughts and emotions on which you will take action (useful and productive thoughts...even creative thoughts).

When it comes to processing our thoughts, we tend to repeat the same old patterns instead of creating new ones. But there is only one person who is in control of those internal thought patterns... and that person is you. The more you increase your awareness of the thoughts being produced by your Lower Mind and the more you quickly process and let go of those useless thoughts... the more you can leverage the elongated spaces between these thoughts to generate more positive and creative thought processes from your Higher Mind perspective.

Our Higher Mind is a virtual unlimited resource that remains untapped by most people. The reason for this is quite simple. They spend all their their time and energy entertaining useless and wasteful thoughts created by their Lower Mind. As a result, no elongated spaces of time are being created where these Higher Mind thought processes can occur.

The more we embrace these elongated spaces and the more we leverage the creative aspects of our Higher Mind...the more we will see our personal potential escalate.

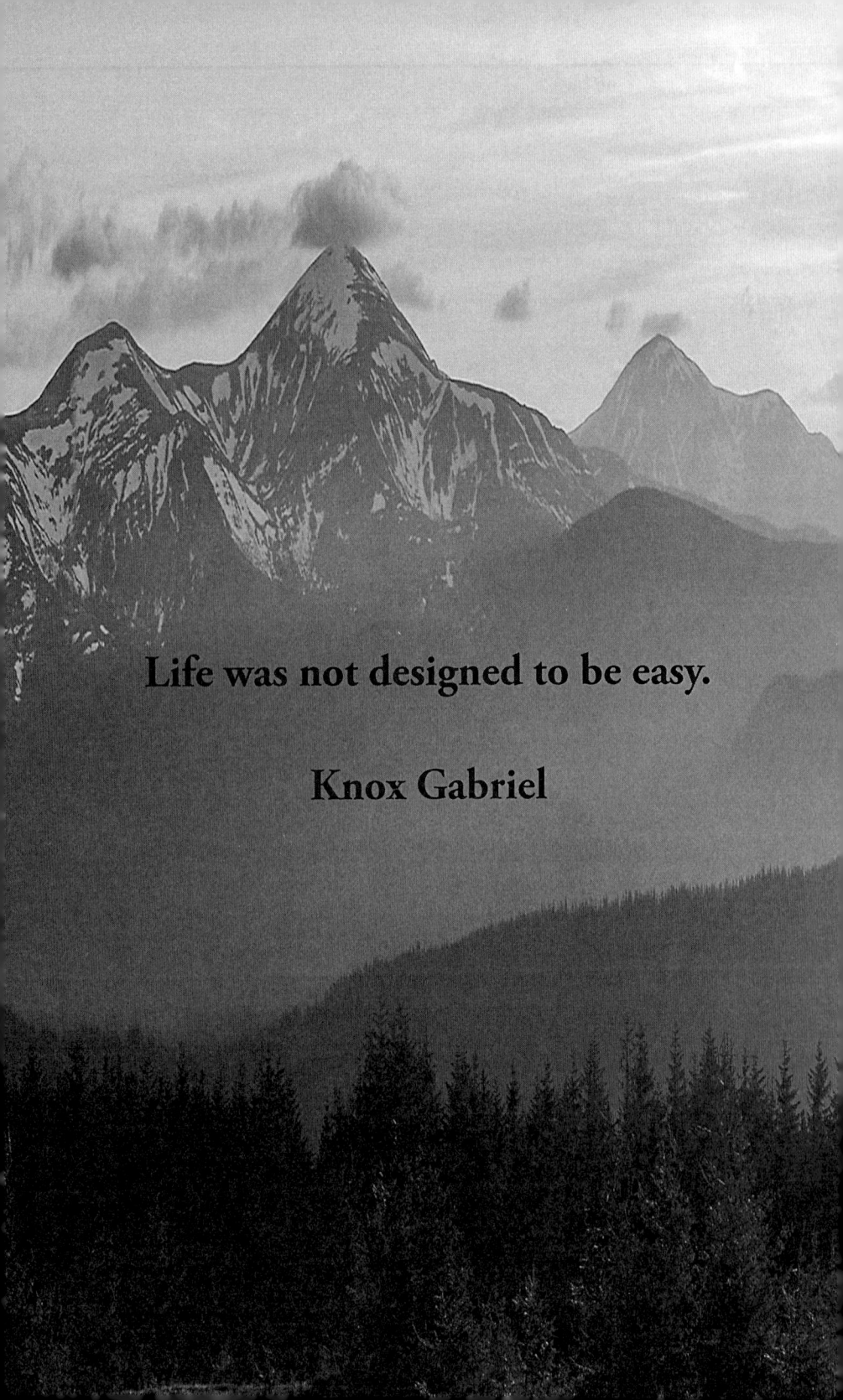

Life was not designed to be easy.

Knox Gabriel

Learning From Life

As you become more aware of the thoughts created by your Lower Mind and begin learning how to quickly process and let go of these thoughts, you eventually learn to process life events differently. It doesn't change the fact that some of these life events are still difficult to go through but it does change how you handle yourself during these events.

But you may still find yourself asking "How can I be at rest and at peace while I'm going through painful and traumatic life events?"

Let me ask you a question. Why is it that long after we go through a negative life event (even with all it's pain and trauma) we always look back on this event as one of the most real and valuable experiences of our life? If this experience is part of the natural rhythm of life…then why shouldn't it be something that we accept and embrace during the process of going through this experience?

There are two things that keep us from taking this "higher" approach to these experiences:

1. The thoughts and emotions created by our Lower Mind.

2. Our attitude and perspective toward life in general.

In the previous sections, we focused on how to more effectively process the thoughts and emotions created by our Lower Mind. So, we've already addressed the first of these two items.

In regards to the second item, most of us have an entirely misplaced attitude and perspective toward life in general. Our attitude is that life should always be easy… and when things are not easy there is something wrong in our life. Our perspective is that life was designed to be easy and that other people and other events are always messing up the natural design of your life.

Life was not designed to be easy.

Why Is Life So Hard?

To even ask this question is a clear indicator that you have a misplaced perspective on life. Life was never designed to be easy and free from traumatic events.

If you take a step back from your own life. Then take a few more steps back to the original creation of our universe. It is clear that our universe was not designed or created to always be in a state of calmness. In fact, there are many properties of our universe that are specifically designed to support catastrophic events as a normal part of the rhythm but not to allow these events to destroy our universe as a whole. We have many galaxies, stars, planets and loose fragments (asteroids) which are always in motion. Inevitably, there are random events that occur which can trigger catastrophic events. Yet all of this was designed and created to be a natural part of the rhythm of life in our universe.

In the same way, our lives were never designed to always be easy and free from traumatic events. Our lives were designed to have a consistent rhythm of positive and negative events. The fact that both negative and positive events happen in our life is what keeps our life in balance. If all we ever had were positive events in your life, we would become so egotistical, arrogant, complacent, lazy and insufferable that we could not stand to be around each other. We would end up killing each other (which in a weird way would restore the natural order back to life in the way originally intended because we would obviously begin experiencing negative events again at that point).

When you ask the question "Why is life so hard?" you are clearly indicating that you don't have an understanding that "hard" is a perfectly normal part of life. Furthermore, these "hard" events that occur have just as much importance and value in your life as the "easy" or "happy" events.

If you believe in a divine Creator of the universe, then it is clear that the Creator knew in advance that both positive and negative events would occur in our lives. This is further evidenced by many of the properties that He designed and created within us to handle these types of events. Our physical body, our mind and our emotions all have specific properties that were designed to equip us to handle painful and traumatic events in life.

The Difference Between Pain and Suffering

If we were never intended to experience painful and traumatic life events, then why were our bodies and minds designed in such a way to be prepared for painful events?

Pain is a natural feedback mechanism that was built into our bodies, minds and emotions. When our physical body encounters something that could possibly damage it, the nerve endings throughout our bodies are designed to send signals to our brain which triggers our natural defense mechanisms (i.e. pulling away from a sharp or hot object). Our minds are also designed to handle pain. When our body sends pain signals to the brain, our mind triggers the release of chemicals (such as adrenalin) which assists our body in dealing with the pain.

Even our emotions were designed to experience painful and traumatic events. If we were not intended to experience pain and trauma, then why were we created with the natural emotions of fear, anger, sadness or shame. Even the muscles in our face were specifically designed to express these emotions (which, by the way, is a universal trait which crosses all cultural, religious and geographic boundaries).

Pain is not only a natural part of your life…it can also be a beautiful part of your life. The pain that you feel when someone breaks your heart is an expression of the love that you had for that person. The intense pain that you feel after the death of a loved one is a further expression of the deep love you had for that person.

As you can see from these examples, pain is a natural, valuable and beautiful part of your life. You should never think of your life as something that will be free from pain. In fact, you should expect and even anticipate pain that will occur in your life. However, you should also realize that pain is a temporary thing when handled properly in your life. It comes and then it goes away as your body and your mind heals naturally.

On the other hand, suffering is a different thing. Suffering is something that is entirely created by your Lower Mind. Suffering is not a natural part of you. You were never designed or created to suffer for extended periods of time. Most of the things that you consider to be "hard" in life are the results of things you create in your Lower Mind. This is just another form of ignorance that you must overcome.

The only thing that keeps you from being free from suffering is the thoughts and emotions created by your Lower Mind. We've already discussed many examples of the different types of useless and wasteful thoughts generated by your Lower Mind. These are exactly the types of thoughts that create suffering in your life. The more you entertain all these thoughts and emotions, the more you will suffer through life's experiences.

However, suffering is not a requirement…it is a choice. If you choose to entertain the thoughts and emotions created by your Lower Mind then you are "choosing" to suffer. There is nothing wrong with experiencing emotions associated with certain valid thought processes. We've already talked about how it is normal to allow yourself to briefly experience these painful emotions as you quickly process the thoughts created by your Lower Mind. However, when you choose not to process these thoughts quickly… when you choose to hold on to these painful emotions… this is when you are choosing to inflict suffering upon yourself.

You will know that you are inflicting suffering upon yourself when you hear yourself thinking or making statements like:

- "I hate this".
- "This blows".
- "I wish this wasn't happening".
- "I don't deserve this".
- "These people are such idiots".

All of these statements are indicators that you are not only entertaining your Lower Mind thoughts but are, in fact, holding onto and perhaps embellishing on these thoughts. Furthermore, making these statements indicates that you are still living your life from the perspective that you should never experience negative or difficult events in your life (as we discussed in the previous section).

While you are certainly going to experience pain in your life, the only thing that keeps you from being free from suffering... is yourself.

Using Death As A Reference Point

When you think of pain and suffering, you often think of events in your life which have involved death (either the death of someone you knew or perhaps a near death experience for yourself). But just as pain can be a beautiful thing in life... death can also be a beautiful thing in your life. Death plays a valuable and important role in your life. While it can be an extremely painful experience when someone you know and love passes away...there are often many positive things that come out of these experiences as well.

While death is certainly traumatic, it is still just another of a series of events in our life. The amount of suffering that is associated with death is determined by how you process this event in your life. If you are constantly holding onto the negative thoughts and emotions associated with death created by your Lower Mind... then you will inflict upon yourself great suffering associated with a death event. However, if you use a more healthy approach (by processing the event as quickly as possible and letting go) then you can minimize the suffering associated with the event. This is not to say that you shouldn't process and feel the emotions associated with death. There is a natural and healthy grieving process associated with death. But holding onto these emotions indefinitely will only inflict unwarranted suffering in your life.

But what role does death play in your own life. Most people go through life being afraid of death. But why are you so afraid of death?

Is it because you think you still have more living you want to do? If so, then why don't you do more living each and every day? Why do you spend so much time planning for all the things you want to do "some day" rather than actually doing them?

You shouldn't be afraid of death…you should be afraid of not living!

Your body is decaying and getting older every single day. Before you know it…you will be in that very moment where death is ready to take you. It doesn't matter what event you are currently experiencing in life… there are people who have died doing exactly what you are doing today. Death is no respecter of age, gender, race, religion or any situation. Babies, children, teens, adults and seniors die every single day.

What would you do if you only had 1 week to live? What would you do with your last week alive? Why aren't you living that way now? How much of your time are you wasting on meaningless things? Why wait for your last week of life when there are 52 weeks in every year? Why wait for the last day of your life when their are 365 days every year? All the things you pay attention to and spend so much time focusing on will be gone in an instant (all your material things, wish list and dreams in life). If all these things can be gone in an instant…then why do you spend so much of your time focusing on them?

Why spend so much time worrying about the next event in your life (or trying to avoid the next event in your life)? This is just your own fears keeping you from experiencing life. Make a decision to take action. Do the things you haven't done. Say the things you haven't said. Don't worry about what will happen next. Whatever it is… you are prepared to handle it.

People who are truly aware and living from their Higher Mind live this way all the time (at least most of the time). You can spot them immediately by the way they live their lives and interact with others. They live in the moment for every moment.

There is no teacher greater than death. Death is not a morbid thought. It is the greatest reference point you can use to live life in a more aware and abundant way.

When you live your life with death as your reference point, you become that bold, truly aware person that everyone admires and wants to be like. Living life with no regrets. Never having to worry about when you're going to die because you're living life to the fullest every day.

It is your total willingness to experience life's events (both positive and negative) that gives your life meaning. It is your willingness to live in each moment and let that moment fill you up completely that provides this meaning. Whether you are simply walking outside… or sitting in your favorite chair reading this book… or watching your child from across the room… or talking to your parent or grandparent… embrace every aspect of each moment. Embrace what you see, what you hear, what you smell, what you feel in that moment and let it resonate throughout your whole being. This is something you will have to consciously practice. Since you don't do it regularly it will seem odd at first. But the more you practice it… the more moments you capture in this way… the more meaningful and fulfilled your life will be.

When you are not living in the moment you are just focusing on future moments you would like to experience. All the other things you focus on are just you trying to search for meaning. It is not your desire for a particular event that matters. It is not even your desire to fulfill your bucket list that matters. It is your willingness to take life as it comes to you each and every day and enjoy every aspect of having new experiences. It doesn't matter whether they are positive or negative experiences. You need to embrace them and accept them as part of your life.

Life's events will never stop. As you have seen from our study of people's lives… the rhythm of life never stops. You don't need to change your life. You just need to change you. Change the way you view life and the way you experience life. Change the way you process your thoughts and emotions. Embrace them, experience them and then let them go!

If the events in your life are getting you down, go spend some time at a cemetery and contemplate death. Go visit a crematory and think about all the bodies that no longer have life left in them and are nothing but ashes. Then focus your mind on being grateful that you have the freedom and opportunity to experience each and every event in your life. Be grateful that you have time left to recover from whatever events have happened in your life and start focusing on appreciating and living every moment. If you have to, do this weekly until you learn to live in the moment and experience life to the fullest every day.

Embracing Life

This is not to say that all things in your life have to be viewed as being equally good. It is just saying that if you learn to appreciate the process of life… the rhythm of life… then you will embrace and value each of your experiences (both positive and negative). Furthermore, when other people observe you going through these experiences with the grace and power of someone who has become fully aware and conscious of the power that resides within your Higher Mind…they will naturally be drawn to you and want to know more about how you are able to go through life in this manner.

Just as people are drawn to you because of your increased awareness you'll find yourself wanting to spend time with other "aware" beings. You will begin to be more selective in who you choose to closely associate yourself. You will begin to become acutely aware of just how unevolved and unaware most people are as it relates to these principles. While you will feel grateful that you now see life differently, you will still feel compassion for those who have yet to discover these principles. You will naturally gravitate toward people who view life in the same way you do.

There are literally millions of people who need to hear and understand these principles. This fact may play an important role in helping you identify and establish your new or renewed purpose in life (which we will discuss later in this course).

Using The Rewind Button In Your Life

One of the most valuable aspects of using the LifeTracers process to chart your life is the fact that it makes it easy to view your life in ways you never have before.

When you start taking a closer look at your life, it is common to ask yourself the question "How did I become this person that I am today"? Let's face it. Many of us have become a little jaded, judgmental or perhaps even angry about life in general. Perhaps you are just disappointed, disillusioned or lost faith in what life has to offer you. Regardless of where you are mentally and emotionally today, there is a process you can use to give yourself a renewed perspective on life.

If you go to your LifeTrace chart and look at the point in time where you are today on your chart. Then begin to "press the Rewind button" on your life. Continue holding the Rewind button until you get back to the point on your chart before your very first life event. For most of us, this will mean that we are back to our childhood again.

> *"When I was a child, I talked like a child,*
> *I thought like a child, I reasoned like a child. "*
> *1 Corinthians 13:11 - New International Version*

Before we experienced our very first life event, our perspective on life was untainted by all the events that would happen in our life. Our mind was a clean slate with nothing but positive hopes and dreams for the future. In affect, we had the "faith of a child". This is a beautiful way to experience life… going through life enjoying each moment of every day without the negative thoughts and emotions which weigh us down and alter our perspective on life.

The only problem is that, as a child, we also lacked the "awareness" of the fact that life events would eventually happen in our life. We also lacked the awareness of how we should process these events when they happened to us.

From this point in our life, we can begin to "press the Play button" in our lives but be ready to "press Pause" after each life event on our LifeTrace chart. After each life event, we can ask ourselves the following key questions:

- How did I process the thoughts and emotions associated with this event? Did I process them quickly and let go of them or did I hold onto them?

- How long did I hold onto those thoughts and emotions after the event?

- How many of those thoughts and emotions do I still carry with me today?

- How did this event (and the associated thoughts and emotions) change me from my initial perspective as a child?

As we go through this process of examining each event in our life (and the associated thoughts and emotions) we can clearly begin to see how we have become the person we are today. Some of us carry deep-seated fears that are associated with events that happened earlier in our life. Some of us carry anger associated with one or more events. Some of us carry disappointment, disillusionment or perhaps shame because of previous life events.

Finally Letting Go

This is your opportunity to finally let go of all those thoughts and emotions you've been carrying with you from previous life events. You should set aside an entire day (or perhaps a weekend) to use your "Rewind", "Play" and "Pause" buttons to slowly go through your life re-processing each event one by one:

- Take a step back and a step up and position yourself in your objective Higher Mind.

- Think about the details of each event (as much as you can remember). Try to think the same thoughts you did at the time of the event. Then feel the same emotions you did when the event occurred. Let those emotions resonate within your Lower Mind for just a few moments. Feel the anger. Feel the disappointment. Feel the sadness. Feel the shame.

- Then let them go! Let them go and feel those thoughts and emotions pass out of your Lower Mind. Feel the energy released from your body when you let them go.

- Now move on to the next event and process it the same way. Remember, the goal is to restore your mind back to a "clean slate" where your mind and emotions are at peace with these events.

Some of these events may be harder than others to let go of. But you must remain committed to the goal of restoring your perspective on life to a clean slate... to free yourself of all the emotional baggage that keeps you from living a joyous and fulfilled life today.

From time to time, future events may even cause some of these past thoughts and emotions to resurface. You can use this same formula to "reprocess" those events and then let go of them.

You were not born hating others.
You must learn to hate.
If you can learn to hate,
then you can re-learn to love.

Knox Gabriel

UNDERSTANDING OTHERS

In the previous chapters, we explored the process you should go through to understand your own true identity. We discussed the importance of coming to the realization that you are a complete and perfect creation. We also learned how to use the "Rewind" button in your life to go back and examine how your life events have changed your perspective on life since you were a child.

If you find these principles and processes valuable and useful for understanding yourself...then you must also apply these same principles and processes when trying to understand others. When you look at other people and the person they have become... you are really just looking at a reflection of yourself. We were all created by the same creation process. We all started life as a baby inside the womb. We all started off as a clean slate mentally and emotionally. We were all equipped the same way to handle pain and traumatic experiences. The more you can come to see yourself in others... the more success you will have in understanding others and becoming empathetic to their perspective on life.

If you took two small girls from two different parts of the world and raised them in the same culture, same environment and exposed them to the exact same life events... you would find that they share many similarities in their perspective on life. While they would not be identical (because they would still have certain personality differences) they would share many of the same viewpoints towards other people and would most likely carry with them much of the same emotional baggage. They would also share similar identities (the way they view themselves) and would most likely process life events in similar ways. If you interviewed each of them at age 50 you might be surprised how closely they resemble each other (even though they came from two different parts of the world).

So, why is it that you look at people from different parts of the world so differently than yourself? The truth is they are not that different from you at all. They all started their life the same way you did. What has caused them to become different is the culture, environment and life events they have experienced. If you were to look at their LifeTrace chart and then use the "Rewind" button to go back to the beginning of their life, you would then be able to use the "Play" and "Pause" buttons to slowly walk through their life and see how each of their life events has caused them to develop a certain perspective on life and on other people.

Let's start by looking at people who are raised in a different religious and spiritual environment than you. Does this make them "wrong" just because they have different religious or spiritual beliefs? Remember, (as we discussed previously) beliefs are just choices each of us has made in our life. Beliefs are not facts and they are not truth. They are simply beliefs. If we could prove them to be true they would no longer be beliefs. So to look at another person and say they are "wrong" just because they have chosen different beliefs… is just a sign of your own ignorance about beliefs.

Don't get me wrong. This doesn't mean you have to agree with their beliefs. But you must respect the fact that they used a similar process as you did to determine their beliefs. They were just in a different environment or culture and had different influences in their life. Since most people merely adopt the given religion of their family or culture it is unlikely that their process was much different than yours.

[Note: The exception to this would be the small percentage of people on the planet who have actually gone on a journey to explore and discover their personal beliefs (including the study of all major world religions). But this is a very small percentage of people and they are spread all over the world.]

So, let's take a rather extreme example and evaluate it in more detail. If you are from the United States (or one of the countries closely aligned with the U.S.) you may have a certain amount of disdain, anger or hatred for terrorists who have conducted heinous acts around the world. You might even say "they are evil". But what if I told you that you are just as capable of conducting similar heinous or evil acts. I know you think I am crazy for even proposing this line of thought… but bear with me.

If you were to take any single one of these individual terrorists and complete a LifeTrace chart on them, you would be able to "Rewind" back to the beginning of their life and begin to examine each event that has happened to them. You would also have to take into account the emotional impact each of these events had in their life and how many of these thoughts and emotions have been locked up inside of them. In addition, you would find that at some point they were introduced to a set of beliefs which includes violence as an acceptable way to right the wrongs against them.

You are probably still saying to yourself that there is no way you could go down that path and conduct those types of heinous acts. But now imagine watching your entire family killed by a missile that fell on your house. Then your spouse was dragged into the streets and taken off to a secret destination for "questioning" and is eventually returned all beaten (or perhaps never returned at all). Furthermore, all of these acts are conducted by a nation which follows a different religion or set of beliefs than you do…and they clearly believe in violence as a means for righting the wrongs they feel were committed against them. Now apply some peer pressure from all of your high school or college friends who are joining forces to actually do something about all these terrible things you've experienced in your life.

So, are you still saying to yourself that you would sit there and do absolutely nothing to avenge the death of your family? Would you at least harbor anger or hatred in your heart for what they did to your spouse? Would you feel compelled to follow your own religious beliefs (which clearly condones and perhaps even rewards standing up for your own people) and join a group of fellow believers to do something about these wrongs?

Keep in mind that many world religions (including Islam and Christianity) have a long history of condoning and rewarding violence as an acceptable method for righting wrongs. Even King David ("the man after God's heart") was a mighty warrior and led a great army which devastated neighboring nations and villages. The United States itself is arguably the strongest military power in the world and certainly no stranger to using violence to right the wrongs they feel have been committed against them (even in situations where the motives turn out to be questionable).

The point of this discussion is certainly not to try to justify one form of violence over another. The point here is to put yourself in the shoes of other people around the world and begin to understand how they are not so different than we are. Given the right set of circumstances, the right set of life events and the right cultural influences each of us is equally capable of conducting heinous acts against other people. The one thing that can save us from becoming one of these types of people is to become more aware and more evolved in how we process life events as they happen to us. The more we can learn to step back and observe our thought processes... the more we can learn to quickly process thoughts and emotions. The faster we can learn to let go of these negative emotions the better off our planet and all the people around us will be.

Learning to recognize yourself in other human beings is the beginning to a rewarding journey of self-exploration. To see yourself in others (or to see them within you) requires you to expand your own sense of identity. Each of us is part of the same creation process and therefore we are all connected in multiple ways. You are not just a single self… you are part of a global humanity.

If you are always viewing others as something separate from yourself, why would you bother trying to understand them. If you will take the time to understand them you will also learn something very valuable about yourself.

When you begin to see others as someone who is connected to you (or better yet a part of you) you will approach them much differently. If you are having a hard time seeing others as yourself, then you must expand your view of not only who you are…but who they are as well.

This is not to say that all beings are equally good or equally aware (because they are not). But you have the same fundamental capacities that they do. Each person is just a different variety of the same form of humanity.

Keep in mind, this doesn't mean you have to agree with their actions, beliefs or perspectives. But you should have an understanding of how they came to develop these beliefs or perspectives which fuel their actions. This is the first step in creating a common ground where we can all learn to coexist in a universe that created us all in the same way.

Next Steps

In this step, we have gone inside your mind to examine how you process your thoughts and emotions and how you can learn to process your thoughts and emotions in a more effective and efficient way. You have also learned how to stay calm and centered while you are going through difficult life events. Finally, you learned how to use the "Rewind" button to understand how you have become the person you are today and how to use the "Rewind | Play | Pause" to go back and reprocess life events and let go the many thoughts and emotions you carry with you to this day. Perhaps most importantly, you learned how to use this same ""Rewind | Play | Pause" process to understand others more effectively.

In Step 4, we are going to combine everything you've learned in the first three steps to actually start creating a specific plan for the remainder of your life. A plan which will show you how to create a true life of significance and to leave a legacy which will impact the lives of people for generations.

I'll see you in the next step.

Knox